engage

Level 1

Workbook

Alistair McCallum

Welcome back

1 Look at these pictures. Fill in the blanks with *I, you, he, she, it, we* or *they*.

1 *She* is my sister.

2 _____ is my brother …

3 and _____ are our parents.

4 Hi! _____ are Japanese.

5 This is my car. _____ is beautiful!

6 Excuse me. Do _____ speak English?

7 Yes. _____ am from London!

2 Look at Duarte's family tree, then fill in the blanks with the words below.

~~brother~~ father grandparents mother sister

Jose = Carmen

Ramiro = Yelena

Marcos   Duarte   Izabel

"Hi! I'm Duarte. I'm from Brazil. Marcos is my
(1) ___*brother*___ . Izabel is my (2) _____.
Ramiro is my (3) _____ . Yelena is my
(4) _____ . Jose and Carmen
are my (5) _____ ."

3 Fill in the blanks. Use the affirmative (✓) or negative (✗) of *be*.

1 My name ___*is*___ Pedro. I _____ Mexican. ✓

2 Tania and Rose are at home. They _____ at school. ✗

3 I'm a student. I _____ a movie star! ✗

4 Danny _____ my friend. We _____ in the same class. ✓

5 My sister is three years old. She _____ a student! ✗

4 Unscramble the days of the week and put them in the correct order.

1 _Monday_   5 _____
2 _____   6 _____
3 _____   7 _____
4 _____

adurasty   awendedys   hatursdy   ~~dymona~~
yasdun   yirdaf   uaysdet

5 These are six months of the year. Add the missing six months, and put them in the correct order.

1 _January_   5 _____   9 _____
2 _February_   6 _____   10 _____
3 _____   7 _____   11 _____
4 _____   8 _____   12 _____

May   November   March
July
September   ~~January~~

6 Fill in the blanks with the verbs below. Use the imperative form, affirmative (✓) or negative (✗).

| be | come | have | go | play |

1 The lesson starts at 9:00. _Don't be_ late! ✓
2 It's eleven o'clock. _____ to bed! ✓
3 _____ fun at the party tonight! ✓
4 It's late and I'm tired. _____ your CDs! ✗
5 It's my birthday. _____ to my house! ✓

7 Look at the pictures and complete the crossword.

1
2
3
4
5
6
7

Unit 1

Vocabulary

1 Find seven verbs in the word snake. Then fill in the blanks in the phrases below.

1 _dance_ at a party
2 _____ a computer
3 _____ in a movie
4 _____ martial arts
5 _____ French
6 _____ the guitar
7 _____ a motorcycle

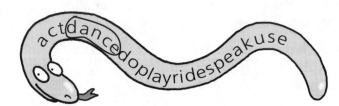

2 What can they do? Fill in the blanks with the words below.

| make clothes | run fast | swim | send a text | water-ski | windsurf |

1 They can _run fast_ .

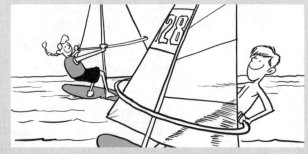

2 They can _____ .

3 She can _____ .

4 He can _____ .

5 He can _____ .

6 She can _____ .

Grammar

1 Who's speaking? Look at the chart and match the sentences with the people.

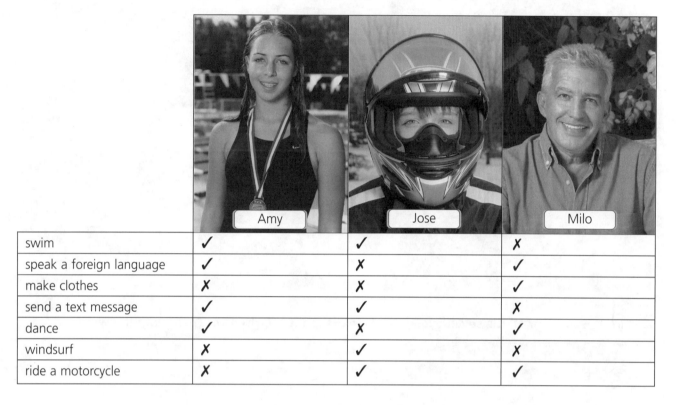

	Amy	Jose	Milo
swim	✓	✓	✗
speak a foreign language	✓	✗	✓
make clothes	✗	✗	✓
send a text message	✓	✓	✗
dance	✓	✗	✓
windsurf	✗	✓	✗
ride a motorcycle	✗	✓	✓

1 "I can't swim."   a Amy and Jose

2 "We can speak a foreign language."   b Jose

3 "I can windsurf."   c Milo

4 "We can't make clothes."   d Amy and Milo

2 Fill in the blanks with *can* or *can't*.

1 Milo _*can't*_ windsurf.

2 Amy and Jose _____ swim.

3 Jose _____ speak a foreign language.

4 Milo _____ dance.

5 Amy _____ ride a motorcycle.

3 Write questions and answers about Amy, Jose and Milo.

1 Amy and Jose / make clothes

   Can Amy and Jose make clothes ?   _No, they can't_ .

2 Amy / dance

   _____ ?   _____ .

3 Milo / send a text message

   _____ ?   _____ .

4 Jose and Milo / ride a motorcycle

   _____ ?   _____ .

Vocabulary

1 **Look at the pictures, then circle the correct word.**

1 They have (short) / long hair.
2 She has straight / wavy hair.
3 He has a moustache / beard.
4 She has small / big eyes.

2 **Circle (→ or ↓ or ↘) the seven eye and hair colors in the wordsearch. Then write the words.**

A	N	A	G	G	R	T	O
B	E	M	L	R	I	U	D
R	L	H	C	A	E	R	Y
O	V	A	E	Y	T	E	D
W	U	Y	C	N	S	D	N
N	O	E	R	K	T	Y	I
A	R	B	L	U	E	T	S
C	Y	S	B	L	O	N	D

___black___   _____

_____   _____

_____   _____

_____

3 **Look at the pictures, then fill in the blanks with the correct words.**

Extend your vocabulary

	Ricky is an actor. He isn't (1) ___short___. He's (2) _____. He has (3) _____ hair and he's (4) _____.	good-looking curly ~~short~~ tall
	Anna is a gymnast. She has (5) _____ hair. She's (6) _____. She isn't (7) _____. She can run, jump, and dance.	dark brown overweight slim
	Jim is a weightlifter. He's very (8) _____. He doesn't have any hair – he's (9) _____ !	bald strong

6

Grammar

1 What is Elizabeth saying? Look at the photo of her family, and complete the sentences.
Use *is*, *are*, *have* or *has*.

My Family

Tony (my dad)
and me

Rita (my mum)

My little sister
Sara

Ruth and Arnold
(my grandparents)

Uncle Roy

1 Rita is my mom. She __is__ slim. She _____ wavy hair.

2 Ruth and Arnold are my grandparents. They _____ gray hair.

3 Sara is five years old. She _____ cute!

4 Tony is my dad. He _____ a moustache.

5 Tony and Rita aren't short. They _____ tall.

6 Uncle Roy _____ bald.

7 My name's Elizabeth. I _____ short black hair.

2 Circle the correct words.

1 Rita **(doesn't have)** / **don't have** straight hair.

2 Tony **isn't** / **aren't** short.

3 Elizabeth and her father **doesn't have** / **don't have** blond hair.

4 Rita and Tony **isn't** / **aren't** overweight.

3 These sentences are wrong. Write the correct sentences.

1 Rita is short.
   No! She __isn't short__. She __is tall__.

2 Elizabeth has long hair.
   No! She _____ long hair. She has _____.

3 Uncle Roy is slim.
   No! He _____. He _____.

4 Arnold has a beard.
   No! _____. _____.

5 Elizabeth's grandparents have black hair.
   No! _____. _____.

Unit 2

Vocabulary

1 **Match the sentences with the symbols.**

1 It's snowing.

2 It's raining.

3 The wind is blowing.

4 The sun is shining.

a

b

c

d

2 **Complete the verbs.**

1 c _a r r y_ umbrellas

2 d _ _ _ _ the tango

3 w _ _ _ _ fireworks

4 s _ _ on a chair

5 s _ _ _ a song

6 w _ _ _ in the park

7 s _ _ _ in the ocean

8 s _ _ _ _ _ _ _ on the beach

9 c _ _ _ _ _ _ _ _ New Year

3 **Label the pictures with the weather phrases below.**

| It's cloudy. | It's foggy. | It's freezing. | It's stormy. |

1 _It's foggy._

2 _____

3 _____

4 _____

Extend your vocabulary

Grammar

1 Write the *-ing* form of the verbs.

1 write _____writing_____

2 run _____

3 get _____

4 sing _____

5 celebrate _____

6 send _____

2 Circle the correct words.

1 Tim is sleeping. He (**isn't**) / **aren't** doing homework.

2 I **am** / **is** sending a text message.

3 My friends **is** / **are** playing soccer.

4 We **isn't** / **aren't** watching TV. We're studying.

5 You **is** / **are** using my computer!

3 What's Katie saying? Look at the picture, and complete the sentences. Use the present progressive.

Hi, Donna! Come to my house.
(1) We_____'re having_____ (have) fun!
(2) Ricki _____ (play) the
guitar, and (3) Martha _____
(sing)! (4) My friends _____
(dance). Mom and Dad are in the kitchen.
(5) They _____ (make) pizza.
(6) My grandparents _____
(sit) in the yard. It's cloudy, but (7) it
_____ (not / rain).
(8) I _____ (not / do)
homework this evening!

Vocabulary

1 **What are they doing? Fill in the blanks with the verbs below. Use the *-ing* form.**

babysit	do	eat	~~get~~	sleep	talk	wait

07:00	It's seven o'clock. Amy (1) _is getting_ dressed.
08:00	It's eight o'clock. I'm (2) _____ for a bus.
10:00	It's ten o'clock. Mom is (3) _____ on the phone.
13:00	It's one o'clock. Dad is (4) _____ lunch.
18:00	It's six o'clock. Tom is (5) _____ his homework.
19:00	It's seven o'clock. Grandma is (6) _____ the boys.
00:00	It's midnight. The children are (7) _____ .

2 **What is Marco doing? Match the sentences with the pictures.**

1 He's washing his face. _C_
2 He's brushing his teeth. ___
3 He's getting ready for school. ___
4 He's saying "Goodbye" to his mom. ___
5 He's combing his hair. ___

Extend your vocabulary

Grammar

1 Put the words in order to make questions.

1 going / are / where / you ?
_Where are you going_____?

2 your friend / is / watching TV ?
_____?

3 he / is / what / doing ?
_____?

4 dressed / are / getting / they ?
_____?

5 washing her face / Maria / is ?
_____?

2 Write short answers for the questions.

1 Is Jose brushing his teeth?
_No, he isn't____. ✗

2 Are Mom and Dad watching a movie?
_____. ✓

3 Are you getting ready for school?
_____. ✓

4 Is it raining?
_____. ✗

5 Is Maria babysitting her sister?
_____. ✗

6 Are you and Bill doing your homework?
_____. ✓

3 Complete the conversation between David and Sally.

David: Hi, Sally! What (1) _are you doing___? (you / do)

Sally: I'm sitting in the yard.

David: Are (2) _____ a book? (you / read)

Sally: No, (3) _____. I'm reading a magazine.

David: Is (4) _____ her homework? (your sister / do)

Sally: No, (5) _____. She's watching TV.

David: (6) _____ in the yard? (your mom and dad / sit)

Sally: (7) _____. They're eating in the house.

David: (8) _____? (your brother / sleep)

Sally: (9) _____. He's playing a computer game.

David: (10) _____? (the sun / shine)

Sally: Yes, (11) _____!

Unit 3

Vocabulary

1 Find eight verbs in the word snake. Then fill in the blanks in the sentences.

1 I ___hate___ pop music.
2 My sister _____ s English and Spanish.
3 We _____ breakfast at seven o'clock.
4 Robert _____ s in New York.
5 Mom and Dad _____ to the radio in the morning.
6 We _____ jeans on the weekend.
7 Mr. Williams _____ es English at my school.
8 I _____ Saturdays!

hateloveliveeatlistenspeakteachwear

2 Look at the pictures. Fill in the blanks with the correct verbs.

| drink | enjoy | ~~go~~ | learn | like | meet | take |

Every Saturday, I (1) ___go___ to dance class.
I (2) _____ a big bottle of water with me.
It's hot in class.

I (3) _____ our teacher, Luis, and I (4) _____
the classes. We (5) _____ a lot of new dances!

I (6) _____ my friends at dance class. We go to a
restaurant and eat pizza or (7) _____ cola after
the lesson.

Extend your vocabulary

Grammar

1 **Circle the correct words.**

1 I (**meet**) / **meets** my friends on the weekend.

2 Linda **get** / **gets** up at eight o'clock.

3 Martin and Peter **speak** / **speaks** German.

4 We **do** / **does** our homework after dinner.

5 My dad **enjoy** / **enjoys** his job.

6 You **dance** / **dances** really well!

2 **Fill in the blanks with *does* or *doesn't*.**

1 Carla lives in Argentina. She _doesn't_ live in Brazil.

2 Kazuki plays the piano. He _____ play the guitar.

3 I like pop music. I _____ like hip hop.

4 Mom teaches at my school on Monday. She _____ teach on Sunday.

5 The cat sleeps on the sofa. It _____ sleep on my bed.

6 My grandparents watch TV in the evening. They _____ listen to music.

3 **Read about Angela and Mario. Write affirmative and negative sentences.**

Angela

Hi! I'm Angela. I live in Veracruz, in Mexico. I play tennis every day. I speak Spanish and English. I like the beach. I don't like rain!

Hello! I'm Mario. I live in Tampico, in Mexico. I speak Spanish and English. I love computers. I don't like homework!

Mario

1 Angela _doesn't like_ rain. (like)

2 Mario _____ in Tampico. (live)

3 Angela _____ tennis. (play)

4 Mario _____ homework. (like)

5 Angela and Mario _____ in Mexico. (live)

6 Angela and Mario _____ French. (speak)

7 Mario _____ computers. (love)

8 Angela _____ in Tampico. (live)

Vocabulary

1 Do the crossword.

1

2

3

4 (across)

4 (down)

5

6

7

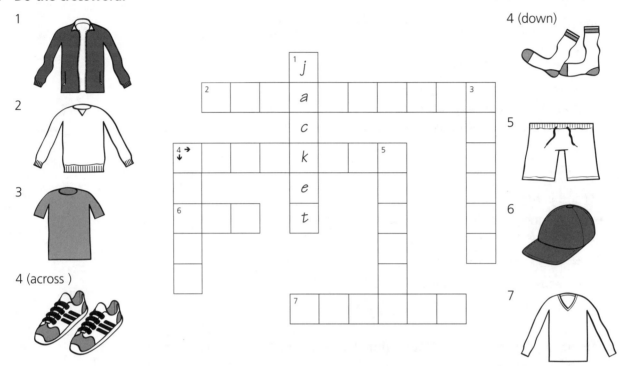

Crossword:
1 (down) j a c k e t

---

2 Fill in the blanks with the words below.

| bathing suit | belt | ~~coat~~ | gloves | hat | sandles | scarf | sunglasses |

It's cold in the winter! I wear a
(1) ____coat____, with a big
(2) _____, (3) _____, and a
long (4) _____.

It's hot in the summer! I go to the beach.
I wear a (5) _____, (6) _____,
(7) _____, and a big
(8) _____!

Extend your vocabulary

Grammar

1 Complete the questions and answers with *do, does, don't* or *doesn't*.

1 _Do_ you listen to rap?   Yes, I _do_ .

2 _____ your friends like hip hop?   Yes, they _____.

3 _____ your mom wear sunglasses?   Yes, she _____.

4 _____ you have a long scarf?   No, I _____.

5 _____ Mr. Jones come from England?   Yes, he _____.

6 _____ Sonja walk to school?   No, she _____.

7 _____ Terry and Mark live in New York?   Yes, they _____.

8 _____ your grandparents write e-mails?   No, they _____.

9 _____ your brother go to university?   No, he _____.

2 You are talking to Tony. Look at the chart and complete the conversation.

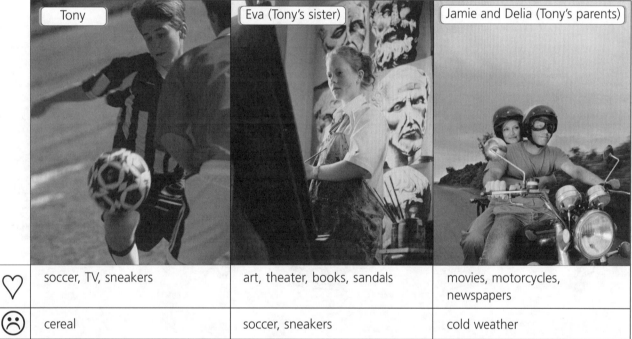

	Tony	Eva (Tony's sister)	Jamie and Delia (Tony's parents)
♡	soccer, TV, sneakers	art, theater, books, sandals	movies, motorcycles, newspapers
☹	cereal	soccer, sneakers	cold weather

You: (1) _Do you play_____ sports? (you / play)

Tony: Yes, (2) _I do_____. I love soccer!

You: Does (3) _____ soccer? (your sister / like)

Tony: No, (4) _____. She hates it!

You: (5) _____ to the theater on the weekend? (your parents / go)

Tony: No, (6) _____. They go to the movies.

You: (7) _____ sneakers? (Eva / wear)

Tony: No, (8) _____. She wears sandals.

You: (9) _____ cereals? (you / eat)

Tony: (10) _____. I hate it!

You: (11) _____ a motorcycle? (Delia / ride)

Tony: (12) _____. Mom and Dad love motorcycles!

Unit 4

Vocabulary

1 **What do these people do? Unscramble the letters and fill in the blanks.**

1 "I ___build___ houses." (dibul)
2 "I _____ food in a restaurant." (okoc)
3 "I _____ cars." (xif)
4 "I _____ planes." (lyf)
5 "I _____ computers." (morgarp)
6 "I _____ the news." (trepro)
7 "I _____ at college." (yusdt)

2 **Look at the pictures. Label the pictures with the words below.**

> cut   explain   fight   save   sell

1 ___sell___   2 _____   3 _____

You write the e-mail address here.

4 _____   5 _____

Extend your vocabulary

Grammar

1 Complete the sentences. Use the present simple.

1 My mom is a doctor. She __works__ in a hospital. (work)

2 I _____ computers in a store in the shopping mall. (sell)

3 My uncle is a builder. He _____ houses. (build)

4 Mr. Davies _____ English at my school. (teach)

5 Arlene and Bruno are American. They _____ in Chicago. (live)

6 Anna is a pilot. She _____ to a lot of different countries. (fly)

2 Look at the picture. Complete the sentences. Use the present progressive.

It's 10:30. Right now Roy and his friends (1) __are__ __studying__ (study) Math.

Janet is their teacher. She (2) _____ _____ (explain) the answer to a question,

and the students (3) _____ _____ (listen).

Donna is a teacher. She isn't teaching at the moment. She (4) _____ _____ (fix) her car!

Vera and Scott are students. Right now they aren't studying. Vera (5) _____ _____ (swim).

She can swim very fast. Scott (6) _____ _____ (sunbathe).

Vocabulary

1 Circle (→ or ↓) the verbs in the wordsearch. Then fill in the blanks in the sentences below.

H	R	X	U	G	R	E	B	S
A	W	C	L	E	A	N	Q	T
V	T	G	O	T	O	B	E	D
E	A	C	L	U	P	L	A	Y
S	L	E	E	P	T	A	V	O
D	K	A	S	R	I	D	E	M

1 I _get up_ at seven o'clock in the morning.

2 I _____ my bike to school.

3 In the afternoon, I _____ my English lesson.

4 I _____ on the phone in the evenings.

5 I _____ _____ _____ at ten o'clock.

6 On Saturdays, I _____ soccer.

7 On Sundays, I _____ my room.

8 I _____ at night.

2 Look at the pictures. Fill in the blanks with *do* or *make*.

1 _do_ the laundry 2 _____ the beds 3 _____ the housework

4 _____ the shopping 5 _____ lunch 6 _____ a phone call

Extend your vocabulary

Grammar

1 **Read these sentences. Check (✓)** *Usually* **or** *Right now*.

		Right now	Usually
1	We go to the dance club on Saturdays.		✓
2	Micky is riding his bike.	✓	
3	I get up at seven o'clock every day.		
4	I'm wearing a white T-shirt at the moment.		
5	We're making the beds.		
6	Dad has lunch at one o'clock.		
7	They do their homework in the evening.		
8	My sister is doing the washing.		

2 **Circle the correct words.**

1 He normally **(goes)** / **is going** to bed at ten thirty.

2 Mom **talks** / **is talking** on the phone at the moment.

3 We **clean** / **are cleaning** our room every week.

4 Right now Terry and Nick **have** / **are having** lunch.

5 I usually **visit** / **am visiting** my friends on weekends.

6 Wendy is at the bus stop right now. She **waits** / **is waiting** for a bus.

3 **Fill in the blanks in Tina's postcard with the verbs below.**
Use the present simple or present progressive.

> celebrate   eat   ~~go~~   have   watch   wear   wear

Hi, Tom!
It's nearly midnight! I usually (1) _go_ to
bed at ten o'clock, but not tonight! I'm
with my friends. We (2) _____
New Year right now. We (3) _____
a good time! I normally (4) _____
TV in the evening, but I'm not watching TV
right now. We usually eat dinner at home,
but tonight we (5) _____
snacks in the park. It's cold! I usually
(6) _____ pyjamas at night,
but right now I (7) _____
a hat and scarf!
Bye!
Tina

Unit 5

Vocabulary

1 Complete the puzzle with restaurant words.

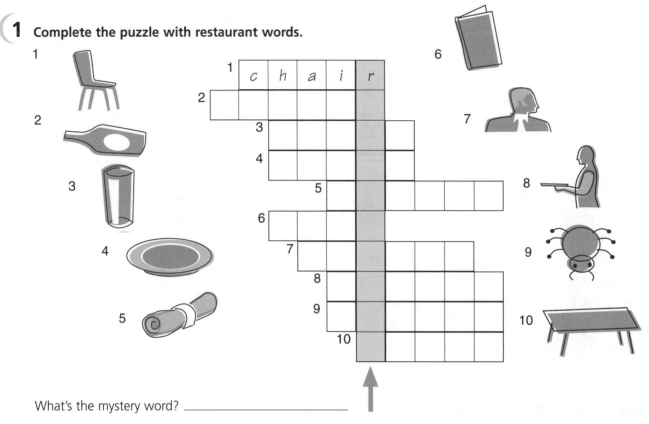

What's the mystery word? _____

2 What is there on the table? Fill in the blanks with the words below.

| bowls | cups | fork | jug | ~~knife~~ | spoon |

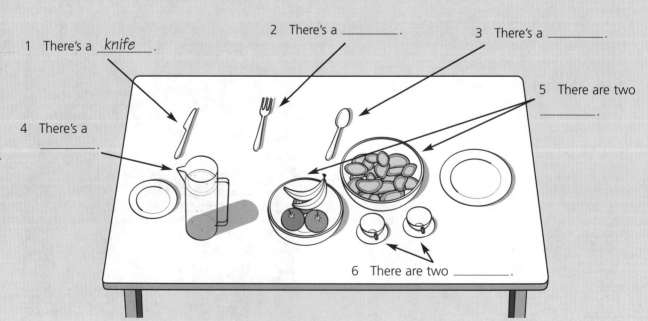

1 There's a _knife_.

2 There's a _____.

3 There's a _____.

4 There's a _____.

5 There are two _____.

6 There are two _____.

Extend your vocabulary

Grammar

1 **Circle the correct words.**

1 There **(is)** / **are** a guitar in my bedroom.

2 There is **a** / **an** umbrella on the chair.

3 There **is** / **are** some people in the classroom.

4 There are two **spoon** / **spoons** on the table.

5 There are **some** / **an** insects on the floor.

6 Are there **a** / **any** cups on the table?   Yes, there are.

7 Is there a bus at the bus stop?   Yes, there **is** / **are**.

2 **Look at the picture. Write affirmative and negative sentences.**

On the table …

1 *There is a bowl*   . (bowl)

2 *There are some cups*   . (cups)

3 _____. (jug)

4 _____. (forks)

5 _____. (spoons)

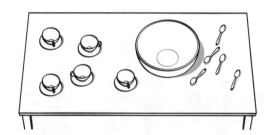

3 **Look at the picture. Write questions and answers.**

In the bedroom …

1 *Is there a clock*   ? (clock)
  Yes, there is   .

2 *Are there any chairs*   ? (chairs)
  No, there aren't   .

3 _____? (CD player)
  _____.

4 _____? (posters)
  _____.

5 _____? (table)
  _____.

Vocabulary

1 Find twelve kinds of food and drink in the word snake. Then write the words below.

___oil___   _____   _____   _____

_____   _____   _____   _____

_____   _____   _____   _____

2 Fill in the blanks with the correct words below.

| fruit juice | milk | orange | salad | ~~sandwich~~ | soup |

I'm hungry! I want …

1 … a ___sandwich___

2 … some _____

I'm thirsty! I want …

5 … some _____

3 … some _____

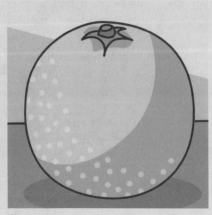

4 … some _____

6 … some _____

Extend your vocabulary

Grammar

1 **Put the words below in the correct column.**

~~apple~~ spoons hamburger bread ~~soup~~ people ~~apples~~
books milk cheese orange water cup oranges
chair

Singular	Plural	Uncountable
apple	apples	soup
_____	_____	_____
_____	_____	_____
_____	_____	_____
_____	_____	_____

2 **Fill in the blanks with *a*, *an*, *any* or *some*.**

1 There isn't _any_ milk in the refrigerator.
2 Give me _____ apple, please.
3 There are _____ students in the classroom.
4 Is there _____ coffee in your cup?
5 There aren't _____ sandwiches in the kitchen, but there is _____ bread.
6 There's _____ table in my bedroom.

3 **Write sentences and questions with the words in the table. Use *there is* and *there are*.**

✓	water	1 There's _some water_ in this jug.
	banana	2 There's _____ in the bowl.
	books	3 _____ on the desk.
✗	menu	4 There isn't _a menu_ on this table.
	apples	5 There aren't _____ in the bag.
	bread	6 _____ in the kitchen.
?	people	7 Are there _any people_ in that house?
	teacher	8 Is there _____ in the classroom?
	milk	9 _____ in the refrigerator?

Unit 6

Vocabulary

1 Look at the photo and complete the body parts.

1 h<u>a</u><u>n</u><u>d</u>
2 a _ _
3 n _ _ _
4 l _ _
5 f _ _ _
6 e _ _
7 h _ _ _
8 e _ _
9 n _ _ _
10 m _ _ _ _

2 Match the words with the body parts below.

| A | eyebrows | | fingers | | lips | | nails | | teeth | | thumb |

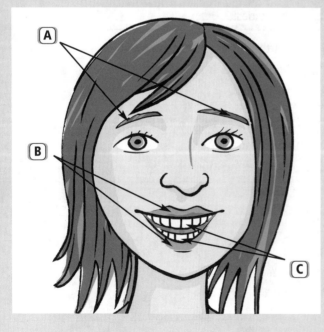

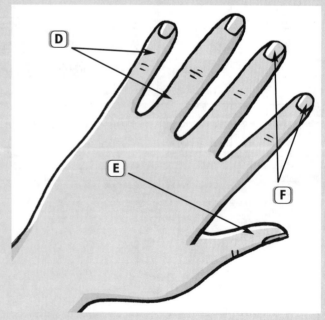

Extend your vocabulary

Grammar

1 **Circle the correct words in the questions and answers.**

1 Whose skateboard **(is)** / **are** this?   **(It's)** / **They're** mine.
2 Whose sneakers are **this** / **these**?   **It's** / **They're** hers.
3 Whose football is **this** / **these**?   **It's** / **They're** theirs.
4 Whose CDs **is** / **are** these?   **It's** / **They're** his.

2 **Match sentences 1–6 with sentences a–f.**

1 They're my DVDs.   a It's his.
2 It's my sister's laptop.   b It's yours.
3 It's my dad's car.   c It's theirs.
4 They're our glasses.   d They're mine.
5 It's your cellphone.   e It's hers.
6 It's Tim and Celia's radio.   f They're ours.

3 **Look at the pictures. Write the questions and Jose's answers.**

1 _Whose_ _watch_ _is_ _this_ ?

2 _It's_ _hers_ .

3 _____ books are _____ ?

4 They're _____ .

5 _____ _____ is _____ ?

6 _____ _____

7 _____ _____ _____ _____ ?

8 _____ _____

Vocabulary

1 Write the opposite of these words in the crossword.

1 light
2 old
3 cheap
4 fast
5 quiet
6 hard

	1 h			2				
	3 e				4			
	a							
	v			5		6		
	y							

2 Fill in the blanks with the adjectives below.

| beautiful | boring | difficult | dry | easy | hard-working | interesting | lazy | ugly | wet |

1 This is a ___boring___ TV program.
It isn't _____.

2 These questions are _____!
They aren't _____.

3 This is a _____ city!
It isn't _____.

Mom, give me that magazine

4 Your T-shirt is _____!
It isn't _____.

5 My mom is _____.
My sister is _____.

Grammar

1 Read about Kimio and Serena. Circle T (true) or F (false).

appearance:	hair – short, black eyes – brown	hair – long, blond eyes – big, blue
dog:	Rex – noisy, young	Millie – lazy, old
computer:	expensive, new	cheap
favorite cars:	small, old	fast, new
loves:	interesting books	beautiful cities
hates:	boring films	wet weather

1 Kimio has blue eyes. T / (F)

2 Serena's hair is long and blond. T / F

3 Kimio has a cheap computer. T / F

4 Serena likes old cars. T / F

5 Kimio loves interesting books. T / F

6 Serena hates dry weather. T / F

2 Put the words in order to make sentences.

1 cities / beautiful / Serena / loves
  Serena loves beautiful cities .

2 short / is / Kimio's / black / hair / and
  _____ .

3 blue / has / eyes / Serena / big
  _____ .

4 Rex / young / is / dog / a / noisy
  _____ .

5 small / car / a / Kimio / old / has
  _____ .

3 Rewrite the sentences about Kimio and Serena.

1 Serena's hair is long and blond.
  She has _long, blond hair._ .

2 Kimio's computer is expensive and new.
  He has an _____ .

3 Serena's dog is lazy and old.
  She has _____ .

4 Kimio has a small, old car.
  His car _____ .

5 Serena has a cheap computer.
  Her _____ .

Unit 7

Vocabulary

1 **Match the words.**

1	suitcases	a	money
2	apples	b	traffic
3	desks	c	time
4	euros	d	baggage
5	months	e	music
6	buses	f	food
7	flights	g	furniture
8	concerts	h	travel

2 **Match 1–6 in the photos with the words below.**

☐ billboard 　1 department store 　☐ road sign 　☐ skyscraper 　☐ sidewalk 　☐ stop light

Grammar

1 **Complete the sentences with *much* or *many*.**

1 How _much_ money do you have?
2 How _____ apples are there in the bag?
3 There isn't _____ traffic in the city today.

4 How _____ CDs does your sister have?
5 There aren't _____ people at the party.
6 Hurry! There isn't _____ time!

2 **Circle the correct words.**

1 There (**is**) / **are** a lot of food in the kitchen.
2 There **isn't** / **aren't** any department stores in this street.
3 I have **a few** / **a little** magazines in my room.
4 There **is** / **are** a lot of students on the bus.
5 I like **a few** / **a little** milk on my cereal.
6 There **isn't** / **aren't** any fruit juice in this bottle.

3 **Look at these pictures, then write questions and answers. Use *how much, not much, not many, how many* and *a lot of*.**

furniture in the room / not much
1 _How_ much _furniture_ is there in the room?
2 There _isn't much_ furniture in the room.

cars in the street / a lot of
3 _____ many _____ are there in the street?
4 There are a _____ cars on the street.

people on the sidewalk / not many
5 _____ on the sidewalk?
6 _____ people on the sidewalk.

baggage in the hall / a lot of
7 _____?
8 _____.

food in the refrigerator / not much
9 _____?
10 _____.

Vocabulary

1 **Unscramble the words.**

Food:

1 _____rice_____ (ceri)

2 _____ (kecchin)

3 _____ (finsfum)

4 _____ (slapep)

5 _____ (eci racem)

6 _____ (urgoty)

Drinks:

7 _____ (ucije)

Cleaning products:

8 _____ (atopestoth)

9 _____ (repap swotle)

10 _____ (posa)

2 **Look at the picture. Then fill in the blanks with the words below.**

| grapes | potatoes | shampoo | steak | tomatoes | toothbrush |

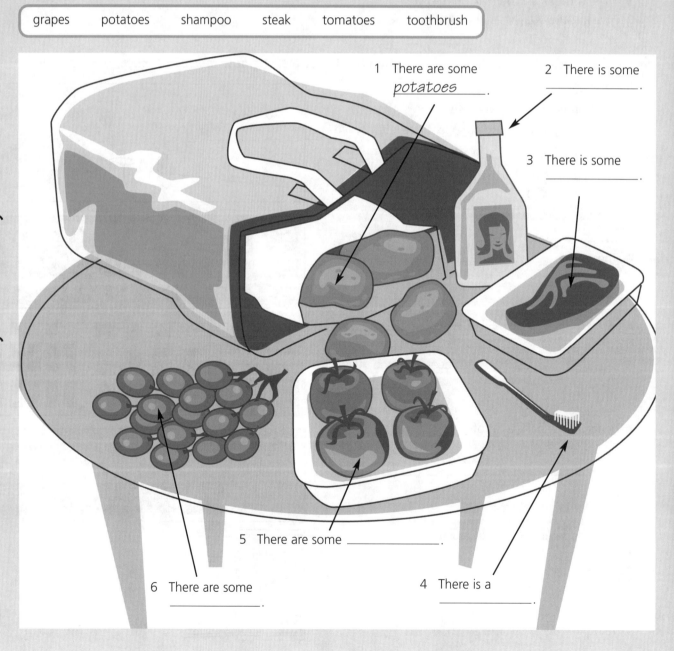

1 There are some
   _____potatoes_____.

2 There is some
   _____.

3 There is some
   _____.

5 There are some _____.

6 There are some
   _____.

4 There is a
   _____.

Extend your vocabulary

30

Grammar

1 Offer these things to your friend. Use *would you like* and *a*, *an* or *some*.

1 _Would you like some juice_ ? (juice)

2 _____ ? (ice cream)

3 _____ ? (money)

4 _____ ? (banana)

5 _____ ? (shampoo)

6 _____ ? (toothbrush)

2 Write the sentences below using the short form.

1 I would like some steak.   _I'd like some steak._

2 He would like a banana.   _____

3 We would like some fruit juice.   _____

4 She would like a yogurt.   _____

5 They would like some grapes.   _____

3 Complete these conversations between Harry and his parents.

Harry: I'm hungry!

Mom: (1) _Would you_ _like_ some fruit?

Harry: Yes, please.

Mom: (2) _____ _____ _____ _____ apple or _____ banana?

Harry: (3) _____ _____ an apple, please.

Harry: I'm thirsty!

Dad: (4) _____ _____ _____ _____ water?

Harry: No, thanks.

Dad: (5) _____ _____ _____ _____ glass of milk?

Harry: (6) _____ _____ great. Thanks!

Unit 8

Vocabulary

1 Circle (→ or ↓) eight nouns in the word search. Then complete the sentences below.

O	P	E	F	A	C	S	O	G	Y	K
S	O	N	G	W	R	I	T	E	R	A
U	L	E	U	K	O	D	I	A	R	D
P	I	B	I	N	V	E	N	T	O	R
E	T	S	T	U	Q	S	A	O	G	U
B	I	R	A	R	T	I	S	T	U	N
Y	C	E	R	X	A	G	R	E	P	N
W	I	M	I	S	H	N	J	I	T	E
P	A	C	S	O	L	E	A	D	E	R
I	N	O	T	V	E	R	P	E	C	L

1 Frida Kahlo was an a*rtist*_____.
2 Newman Darby was an i_____.
3 Jimi Hendrix was a g_____ and s_____.
4 Martin Luther King was a l_____ and p_____.
5 Florence Griffith-Joyner was a r_____ and fashion d_____.

2 Who were they? Fill in the blanks with the correct words.

author	composer	explorer	~~movie director~~	queen	racing driver

1 John Ford was an American *movie director*.

2 Dr Livingstone was an _____ from Scotland.

3 Cleopatra was the _____ of Egypt.

4 Ayrton Senna was a _____ from Brazil.

5 Beethoven was a German _____.

6 Agatha Christie was an English _____.

Extend your vocabulary

Grammar

1 **Circle the correct words.**

1 You **wasn't** / (**weren't**) at school yesterday. **Was** / **Were** you at home?

2 I **was** / **were** born in 1992.

3 Agatha Christie **wasn't** / **weren't** a racing driver.

4 **Was** / **Were** Beethoven an author? No, he **wasn't** / **weren't**!

5 My parents **was** / **were** in America in 2003.

6 **Was** / **Were** you born in Mexico?

Home Page	Holiday photos

Henry's holidays

Switzerland, 1990

Kenya, with Katie, 1993

Greenland, with David, 2000

Ecuador, with Katie and David, 2003

2 **Look at the pictures of Henry and his friends. Fill in the blanks with** *was, wasn't, were* **or** *weren't.*

1 Henry _wasn't_ in Kenya in 1990. He _____ in Switzerland.

2 Henry and David _____ in Greenland in 2000. It _____ very cold!

3 Katie _____ with Henry in 1990.

4 Henry and his friends _____ in Switzerland in 2003. They _____ in Ecuador.

3 **You are talking to Henry. Complete the conversation.**

You: (1) _Were_ you in Kenya in 1993?

Henry: Yes, (2) _____ _____. It (3) _____ hot!

You: (4) _____ _____ with David?

Henry: No, (5) _____ _____. (6) _____ _____ with Katie.

You: (7) _____ Katie and David with you in 2003?

Henry: Yes, (8) _____ _____. We (9) _____ in Ecuador. (10) _____ _____ beautiful!

Vocabulary

1 **Complete the adjectives.**

1 h _a_ ppy

2 s _ d

3 n _ rv _ _ s

4 t _ r _ d

5 s _ rpr _ s _ d

6 b _ r _ d

7 sc _ r _ d

2 **Look at the pictures, then complete the sentences with the adjectives below.**

disappointed   ~~excited~~   jealous   sick   worried

1 It was Christmas. I was
   _____excited_____!

2 I wasn't at school on Monday.
   I was _____.

3 Chris didn't win.
   He was _____!

4 The weather was bad. It was late.
   They were _____.

5 It was the school dance. Meg was with
   my boyfriend! I was _____.

Extend your vocabulary

Grammar

1 Circle the correct words.

1 Dan was disappointed. He was **four** / (**fourth**) in the race.

2 I have **two** / **second** brothers.

3 November is the **eleven** / **eleventh** month of the year.

4 I'm **fifteen** / **fifteenth** years old.

5 I'm really excited. This is my **three** / **third** trip to London.

6 There are **twenty-four** / **twenty-fourth** students in my class.

7 My birthday is on the **one** / **first** of December.

2 Look at the results of the 1000 meters race. Fill in the blanks in the sentences.

1000 meters race: results	
Athlete	**Time (minutes and seconds)**
Linda	2:25
Adele	2:51
Boris	3:02
Christopher	3:11
Zadie	2:18
Martin	2:45
Will	3:02
Mia	2:17

1 Adele was _____fifth_____ .

2 Zadie was _____ .

3 _____ was last.

4 Will and Boris were _____ .

5 Mia was _____ .

6 _____ was fourth.

7 Linda was _____ .

3 Complete the sentences.

1 There are ___seven___ days in a week.

2 New Year's Day is on the _____ of January.

3 There are _____ players in a soccer team.

4 July is the _____ month of the year.

5 There are _____ hours in a day.

Unit 9

Vocabulary

1 Complete the puzzle.

1

2

3

4

5

1 on	f	o	o	t
2 by				
3 by				
4 by				
5 by				

What's the mystery word?   by [ ]

2 Match the transport to the words below.

| helicopter | kayak | subway train | truck | ~~van~~ | yacht |

 **1**

 **2**

 **3**

 **4**

 **5**

 **6**

1 _____van_____

2 _____

3 _____

4 _____

5 _____

6 _____

Grammar

1 **Circle the correct spelling of these words.**

1 Yesterday, I **washd** / (**washed**) the car.
2 The subway train **stopped** / **stoped** at the station.
3 My parents **moved** / **moveed** to this country in 1990.
4 We **carryed** / **carried** the piano to the truck.
5 Darius **traveld** / **traveled** to New York by plane.

2 **Write the simple past of the verbs.**

1 live _____lived_____
2 drop _____
3 cook _____
4 dance _____
5 try _____
6 use _____

3 **Complete the sentences about Bill's day. Use the simple past of the verbs below.**

| arrive | finish | play | start | study | visit | ~~walk~~ | watch |

Last Monday...

morning — college

11:00 to 12:00 — French lesson

2:30 to 4:00 — soccer

evening — grandma's house, TV

Last Monday, Bill (1) _____walked_____ to college in the morning. He (2) _____
at 8:30. At 11:00 he (3) _____ French for an hour. In the afternoon, he
(4) _____ soccer. The game (5) _____ at 2:30 and (6) _____
at 4:00. In the evening, he (7) _____ his grandma. Bill and his grandma
(8) _____ a comedy programme on TV.

Vocabulary

1 Unscramble the letters to make the simple past
form of the verbs. Then write them in the blanks.

1 give   _gave_   (aveg)

2 build   _____ (tubil)

3 meet   _____ (tem)

4 run   _____ (arn)

5 go   _____ (netw)

6 tell   _____ (dolt)

7 spend   _____ (nepts)

8 see   _____ (swa)

2 Look at the pictures. Fill in the blanks with the words below.

> came   did   ~~got up~~   rode   sent

Yesterday …

1 I _got up_ at 7:00.   2 I _____ my bicycle to college.   3 I _____ home at 4:30.

4 I _____ my homework.   5 I _____ an e-mail to my friend.

Extend your vocabulary

Grammar

1 Are the verbs in these sentences in the simple present or the simple past? Write *past* or *present*.

1 I gave my mom a Christmas present.   *past*

2 I live in Mexico.   *present*

3 My dad's a builder. He builds houses.   _____

4 I met my friends yesterday evening.   _____

5 Every day I get up at eight o'clock.   _____

6 Tania ran very fast in the race.   _____

7 I saw a funny programme on TV.   _____

8 We usually leave college at three o'clock.   _____

9 My brother spent a week in England.   _____

2 Fill in the blanks with the simple past form of the verbs below.

> come   do   get up   ~~go~~   meet   see   send   spend

When I was on holiday, I (1) _*went*_ to an
Internet café and (2) _____ an e-mail to my cousin.

Lisa (3) _____ at six o'clock in the morning and
(4) _____ her homework.

Yesterday evening, I (5) _____ a friend, and
we (6) _____ a movie.

Last year, David (7) _____ six months in China.
He (8) _____ home at Christmas.

Unit 10

Vocabulary

1 Unscramble the geographical features and write them in the crossword.

1 steder
2 chabe
3 erriv
4 glujen
5 tinamuno
6 salnid

(crossword)
1 *d*
2 *e*
s
3 *e*
r
5 *t*
6

2 Match the names of these geographical features to the pictures.

cave   ~~lake~~   rainforest   volcano   waterfall

1 In Switzerland there are a lot of mountains and ___*lake*___ s.

2 Costa Rica is beautiful. There are a lot of _____ s.

3 Vesuvius is a big _____. It's near Naples, in the south of Italy.

4 There are some amazing _____ s in Greece.

5 The _____ in Papua New Guinea is amazing. A lot of strange and beautiful birds and animals live there.

Extend your vocabulary

Grammar

1 Read about Steve's visit to London. Put the words in order to make questions.

Last Saturday I went to London with my sister. We went to London because there was a soccer game between Spain and England.
We traveled by train. We arrived at 3:00, and the game started at 3:30. We enjoyed it. Spain won!

After the game we visited grandpa. We ate some cakes. Grandpa gave us some money! Then we went home and watched a DVD. We went to bed late!

1 did / go / last Saturday / Steve and his sister / where ?

_____

They went to London.

2 the game start / did / when ?

_____

At 3:30.

3 they / who / visit / did ?

_____

Their grandfather.

4 eat / they / some grapes / did ?

_____

No, they didn't.

5 at their grandpa's house / did / what / they eat ?

_____

They ate some cakes.

6 did / what / in the evening / they do ?

_____

They watched a DVD.

2 Read the text again and answer the questions.

1 Did Steve go to London with his sister?   Yes, _____ .
2 Did they travel by car?   No, _____ .
3 Did they enjoy the game?   _____
4 Did grandpa give them some money?   _____
5 Did Steve visit some friends in the evening?   _____

3 You are talking to Steve. Complete the conversation. Use the question words and verbs in parantheses.

You: (1) __*Why*__ __*did*__ __*you*__ __*go*__ to London? (Why / go)

Steve: Because there was a soccer game.

You: (2) _____ _____ _____ _____? (How / travel)

Steve: We traveled by train.

You: (3) _____ _____ _____ _____? (When / arrive)

Steve: We arrived at 3:00.

You: (4) _____ England _____ the game? (win)

Steve: No, they didn't. Spain won!

You: (5) _____ _____ _____ _____ in the evening? (What / do)

Steve: We visited grandpa.

You: (6) _____ _____ _____ to bed early? (go)

Steve: No, we didn't. We went to bed late!

Vocabulary

1 Circle (→ or ↓) six verbs in the word search. Then write
the verbs next to their simple past form below.

I	C	R	A	S	H	O	V	S
L	S	E	J	X	I	B	O	T
G	D	V	G	A	T	R	F	Y
D	I	S	A	P	P	E	A	R
R	E	P	W	R	O	A	E	L
O	Q	U	S	I	N	K	L	F

1 _____sink_____ sank
2 _____ hit
3 _____ broke
4 _____ disappeared
5 _____ died
6 _____ crashed

2 Label the pictures with the words below.

~~drought~~   earthquake   fire   flood   hurricane

1 ____drought____

2 _____

3 _____

4 _____

5 _____

Extend your vocabulary

Grammar

1 **Put the words in order to make negative sentences.**

1 watch / my parents / the movie / didn't
   My parents didn't watch the movie.

2 you / wear / didn't / your coat
   _____

3 didn't / any milk / buy / we
   _____

4 didn't / that plate / my sister / break
   _____

5 the fire / I / see / didn't
   _____

6 the tree / didn't / crash into / the car
   _____

7 sink / the boat / in the hurricane / didn't
   _____

2 **Look at this page from Bria's diary. The sentences below are wrong. Write two correct sentences – one negative and one affirmative.**

1 Bria went to the clothes store in the morning.
   She didn't go to the clothes store .
   She went to the music store .

2 She bought three books.
   She didn't _____.
   She bought _____.

3 She spent $200.
   _____.
   _____.

4 Terry and Bria had lunch at 1:00.
   _____.
   _____.

5 Bria played the guitar in the afternoon.
   _____.
   _____.

6 She watched a soccer game in the evening.
   _____.
   _____.

Saturday 10th March

Bria's day

morning: music store — 3 CDs — $20

12:00: lunch with Terry at "Burger Heaven"

afternoon: piano practice

evening: baseball game on TV

Unit 11

Vocabulary

1 Find eight verbs in the word snake. Then write the words in the sentences below.

1 Can I __get__ a cool haircut?
2 Can I _____ my hair green?
3 Can I _____ late tonight?
4 Can I _____ some money?
5 Can we _____ to town in your new car?
6 Can we _____ a party on my birthday?
7 Can I _____ that T-shirt?
8 Can I _____ to the bathroom?

2 What are they asking? Fill in the blanks with the words below.

| go clubbing | go fishing | go shopping | go skiing | go snowboarding | go swimming |

1 ... __go__ __shopping__

Mom! Dad! Can we...

Grammar

1 Choose one phrase from each column to make questions and answers.

(1) Can we go	in the lake?	No way! She's too young.
(2) Can we go skiing	your laptop?	Sorry, he can't. There aren't any seats.
(3) Can Maria drive	to the beach?	I'll think about it, but it's expensive.
(4) Can Jose come	your sports car?	Sorry, you can't. I'm using it today.
(5) Can we go swimming	in Switzerland this Christmas?	Sure you can. It's a beautiful day.
(6) Can I borrow	to the concert with us?	Yes, you can, but be careful – the water is cold!

1 A: _Can we go to the beach_ ?
   B: _Sure you can. It's a beautiful day._

2 A: _____?
   B: _____

3 A: _____?
   B: _____

4 A: _____?
   B: _____

5 A: _____?
   B: _____

6 A: _____?
   B: _____

2 Write questions with the verbs below, and write affirmative (✓) or negative (✗) answers.

> borrow   come   go   have   ~~visit~~

1 A: _Can___ _I___ _visit_ Aunt Jane next weekend? (I)
   B: Sure _you___ _can_. ✓

2 A: Can _____ _____ to my party? (Anna)
   B: Yes, she _____, but ask her parents first. ✓

3 A: _____ _____ _____ some money? (I)
   B: Sorry, you _____. I don't have any. ✗

4 A: _____ _____ _____ snowboarding? (I)
   B: No, _____ _____. It's dangerous! ✗

5 A: _____ _____ _____ a party at our house tonight? (we)
   B: No, _____ _____. I'm tired and your friends are noisy! ✗

Vocabulary

1 Do the crossword.

1 You can get a drink at the coffee _____shop_____ .
2 You can borrow books at the _____.
3 You can see interesting old things at the _____.
4 You can play soccer in the _____.
5 You can go ice skating at the skating _____.
6 There are a lot of rides at the
_____ _____.
7 You can go swimming at the
_____.
8 You can find a lot of different stores
at the shopping _____.

<table>
<tr><td>1</td><td>s</td></tr>
<tr><td></td><td>h</td></tr>
<tr><td></td><td>o</td></tr>
<tr><td></td><td>p</td></tr>
</table>

2 What are they saying? Fill in the blanks with the words below.

| crazy | great | hate | love | not bad | OK | ~~stand~~ | terrible |

What do you think about shopping?

1 I can't _stand_ shopping!
2 I _____ it!
3 It's _____!

4 It's _____.
5 It's _____.

6 It's _____!
7 I _____ it!
8 I'm _____ about shopping!

Grammar

1 Circle the correct words in the requests and responses.

1   A: Let's (**watch**) / **watching** this DVD!
    B: I don't think **it** / **so**. I want to go to bed.

2   A: Why don't we **have** / **having** a cup of coffee?
    B: Let's **no** / **not**. We don't have much time.

3   A: What about **do** / **doing** some homework?
    B: **No** / **Not** way! I'm too tired.

4   A: Let's **go** / **going** to the park!
    B: That's **good** / **a good** idea. We can play soccer.

5   A: What about **visit** / **visiting** the museum?
    B: I don't **think** / **thinking** so. It's boring.

2 Fill in the blanks in these conversations. For each picture, write two suggestions. Write affirmative (✓) and negative (✗) responses.

1   "*Let's go to the amusement park* !"
    (go to the amusement park)
    "*OK*_____. That's a good idea." ✓

2   "What about _____ to the amusement park?"
    "I _____ think so. I want to go home." ✗

3   "Why _____ we _____ your cousin?"
    (visit your cousin)
    "_____. Come on!" ✓

4   "What about _____ _____ _____?"
    "_____ way! I don't want to speak to her!" ✗

5   "_____ make some soup!" (make some soup)
    "That's _____ _____ _____. I'm crazy
    about cooking!" ✓

6   "Why _____ _____ _____ _____
    _____?"
    "Let's _____. I don't know how to cook!" ✗

7   "_____ _____ listening to this CD?"
    (listen to this CD)
    "_____ _____ good idea. I love rock
    music." ✓

8   "_____ _____ to this CD!"
    "I _____ _____ _____. I can't stand
    rock music!" ✗

Unit 12

Vocabulary

1 Complete the puzzle and find the mystery word.

Next summer, we're going to …

1 **s**	**a**	**i**	**l**	a boat

ride a 2 _ _ _ bike

ride a 3 _ _ _

4 _ _ _ a car

5 _ _ _ along the beach

6 _ _ _ _ a kayak

7 _ _ _ _ a mountain

What's the mystery word? (It's another activity!) _____

Extend your vocabulary

2 Match the pictures with the words below.

☐ 3 bungee-jumping	☐ hang-gliding	☐ skydiving
☐ rock-climbing	☐ shark diving	☐ windsurfing

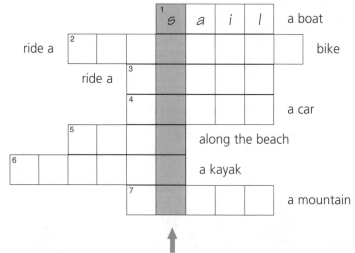

1

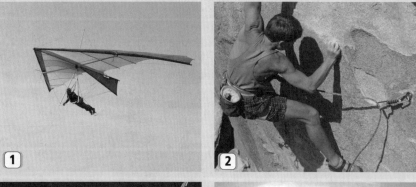

2

3

4

5

6

Grammar

1 Are these sentences about the past or the future? Tick the correct box.

	Past	Future			Past	Future
1 We're going to walk in the park.	☐	✔	5 Kara and Roger are going to visit us.		☐	☐
2 They went to the beach.	☐	☐	6 I had lunch with Marco.		☐	☐
3 You're going to be late.	☐	☐	7 I'm going to go hang-gliding.		☐	☐
4 We rode our bikes.	☐	☐	8 Jessica is going to climb a mountain.		☐	☐

2 Complete these sentences with *am*, *is* or *are*.

1 I *'m*____ going to babysit my sister this evening.

2 Next weekend, Natasha _____ going to buy some new clothes.

3 My friend and I _____ going to go shark diving next year.

4 You _____ going to drive the new car tomorrow.

5 I _____ going to play soccer this weekend.

6 The bus _____ going to arrive soon.

7 Next summer, Micky and Anita _____ going to sail a yacht.

3 Write sentences about the people in the pictures. Use *going to* and the verbs below.

drive to work	get up	play tennis	~~watch TV~~	win the race

1 Simon is *going to watch TV.*

2 Judy _____.

3 Dad _____.

4 Jodie and Mel _____.

5 Kanto and Masuo _____.

Vocabulary

1 Circle (➔ or ⬇) seven verbs in the word search. Then write them in the sentences below.

S	P	E	N	D	I	R	L
T	F	L	R	E	C	Y	P
A	L	O	E	P	O	T	H
Y	E	X	P	L	O	R	E
D	A	T	A	A	Q	E	W
O	V	R	I	N	E	L	P
N	E	C	R	T	U	A	Y
Y	M	N	E	P	T	X	O

1 This is an interesting place. Let's _explore_ it!
2 Don't work too hard. _____!
3 I'm going to _____ a tree in my yard.
4 The taxi's here. Come on – let's _____!
5 We're going to _____ two weeks in Japan.
6 That house is very old. A builder is going to _____ it.
7 I'm going to _____ with my uncle next weekend.

2 Label the pictures with the types of vacation below.

adventure vacation   camping vacation   cruise   hiking vacation   safari   sightseeing tour

1 _adventure vacation_

2 _____

3 _____

4 _____

5 _____

6 _____

Extend your vocabulary

Grammar

1 **Put the words in order to make negative sentences and questions.**

Questions:

1 the cruise / is / stop in the Caribbean / going to ?
Is the cruise going to stop in the Caribbean?

2 talk to her friends / Louisa / is / going to ?
_____?

3 going to / we / where / are / stay tonight ?
_____?

4 are / going to / when / repair the car / you ?
_____?

Negative sentences:

5 aren't / study tomorrow / We / going to .
*We aren't going to study tomorrow*_____.

6 going to / aren't / plant a tree / Tom and Tina .
_____.

7 I'm / enjoy the camping vacation / going to / not .
_____.

8 go on the sightseeing tour / isn't / Dad / going to .
_____.

2 **Read Arthur's plans for next weekend. Write negative sentences with the verbs below.**

Saturday	morning – repair bike
	afternoon – soccer (with Nigel)
	evening – movies (with Angela)
Sunday	morning – beach (with Nigel and Claudia)
	afternoon – homework!
	evening – babysit sister

babysit   play   go   repair   ~~watch~~

1 Arthur and Angela *aren't going to watch* a movie on Sunday.

2 Arthur _____ his bike on Sunday.

3 Arthur and Nigel _____ baseball on Saturday.

4 Angela _____ to the beach with Arthur on Sunday.

5 Arthur _____ his brother on Sunday evening.

3 **You are talking to Arthur. Fill in the blanks in the conversation. Use the words in parentheses.**

You: What (1) _are you going to do_ on Saturday morning? (you / do)

Arthur: I'm going to repair my bike.

You: Are (2) _____ a movie on Saturday? (you / watch)

Arthur: Yes, I (3) _____.

You: Is (4) _____ to the movies with you? (Claudia / come)

Arthur: No, (5) _____.

You: When (6) _____ soccer? (you / play)

Arthur: On Saturday afternoon.

You: (7) _____ on Sunday afternoon? (you / relax)

Arthur: No, (8) _____! I'm going to do my homework!

You: (9) _____ you in the evening? (your friends / meet)

Arthur: No, (10) _____.

Extra reading 1

 OXFORD BOOKWORM STARTERS

Robin Hood

Richard the First is King of England. He is a brave, good man, and the people love him. They call him Richard the Lionheart.

But when the King goes away, his brother Prince John does his work...

Sheriff of Nottingham, the people must pay more taxes!

But Prince John, some of them can't pay.

Then take their houses and animals away from them!

Robin of Locksley lives near the town of Nottingham. He has a big house near Sherwood Forest.

Prince John is a thief! I must do something to help the people without homes or money, Lady Marian.

You're a brave man, but I am afraid for you.

Robin of Locksley is a traitor!

Find him and bring him to me. He must die!

Robin is getting married to Lady Marian Fitzwalter today. Bring him to the castle.

I must tell Robin now.

They want to kill you. You must hide! Don't go home.

How can I marry Lady Marian now? I've got no money, no house. I'm not Robin of Locksley, I'm Robin Hood, the outlaw!

1 Fill in the blanks with words from the box.

> King of England   near a forest
> marry Robin   the King's brother

1 Robin of Locksley lives _____.
2 Richard the First is _____.
3 Lady Marian Fitzwalter wants to _____.
4 Prince John is _____.

2 Circle the correct word.

1 The people of England **love** / **hate** King Richard.
2 Robin wants to help the **rich** / **poor** people.
3 The Sheriff's men burn **Robin's** / **Marian's** house.
4 They can't find Robin. He's hiding in a **church** / **tree**.

3 What do you think? Circle T (True) of F (False).

1 He goes to the forest.   T   F
2 He dies.   T   F
3 He goes to France.   T   F
4 He marries Lady Marian.   T   F

Extra reading 2

Orca

The wind is strong and the boat moves faster and faster. Jack, Max, Sasha and Tonya are happy at sea. There is a lot to do on the boat. The wind is behind them and soon they cannot see England. They are not unhappy now.

They are sailing south. In France they stop at L'Orient and Biarritz. In Spain, they visit La Coruna, and in Portugal they stop in Lisbon. The sun gets hotter and they feel good.

Sasha catches a big fish and they eat it for dinner.

Soon, they are sailing past Africa. Here, everything is different. They stop in Gambia and people look at them. Small children bring beads and shells and cloth. Tonya buys a green hat. There is a lot of colour and noise and excitement.

They sail for weeks and weeks past Africa. They stop at many small towns and villages by the sea. "Africa is so interesting, so big," says Sasha. "It goes on and on. I look at it on the map, but . . ."

"This is why we are here," says Jack. "Talking to different people, seeing different things. The boat, the sea, the wind. Nothing is better than this, is it?"

Some days later they see a big fishing boat. It is moving very fast.

"Hello!" they shout at the boat. The men on the boat look at them angrily. Max looks carefully at the boat through his binoculars.

"There is something wrong with their fishing net," he says. Max moves the binoculars and sees something in the sea. "I can see some net over there." He points to their left. "Why are they leaving it? Let's have a look."

They get nearer to the net and Tonya takes the binoculars.

"What in the world . . ." says Tonya. "What's that? There is something in the net. It's alive, but what is it?"

---

1 Circle the correct word.

1 Jack, Max, Sasha and Tonya are **studying** / **having a vacation** / **working**.

2 They are sailing **south** / **west** / **north** from England.

3 Life on the boat is **boring** / **difficult** / **exciting**.

2 Circle T (True) or F (False).

1 Tonya buys a hat in Spain. T / F

2 The men in the fishing boat want to speak to Max and his friends. T /F

3 The men in the fishing boat leave some net in the water. T /F

3 What do you think is in the net? Tick one answer.

1 A person ☐   2 An animal ☐   3 A boat ☐

Extra reading 3

A Little Princess

One cold winter day a little girl and her father arrived in London. Sara Crewe was seven years old, and she had long black hair and green eyes. She sat in the cab next to her father and looked out of the window at the tall houses and the dark sky.

"What are you thinking about, Sara?" Mr. Crewe asked. "You are very quiet." He put his arm round his daughter.

"I'm thinking about our house in India," said Sara. "And the hot sun and the blue sky. I don't think I like England very much, Father."

"Yes, it's very different from India," her father said. "But you must go to school in London, and I must go back to India and work."

"Yes, Father, I know," said Sara. "But I want to be with you. Please come to school with me! I can help you with your lessons."

Mr. Crewe smiled, but he was not happy. He loved his little Sara very much, and he did not want to be without her. Sara's mother was dead, and Sara was his only child. Father and daughter were very good friends.

"What are you thinking about, Sara?" Mr. Crewe asked.

Miss Minchin was a tall woman in a black dress.

Soon they arrived at Miss Minchin's School for Girls and went into the big house.

Miss Minchin was a tall woman in a black dress. She looked at Sara, and then gave a very big smile.

"What a beautiful child!" she said to Mr. Crewe.

Sara stood quietly and watched Miss Minchin. "Why does she say that?" she thought. "I am not beautiful, so why does she say it?"

Sara was not beautiful, but her father was rich. And Miss Minchin liked girls with rich fathers, because it was good for the school (and good for Miss Minchin, too).

"Sara is a good girl," Mr. Crewe said to Miss Minchin.

"Her mother was French, so she speaks French well. She loves books, and she reads all the time. But she must play with the other girls and make new friends, too."

"Of course," said Miss Minchin. She smiled again. "Sara is going to be very happy here, Mr. Crewe."

1 Fill in the blanks with the name of the country.

> England   India   France

1 Sara's father works in _____.
2 Sara's mother was from _____.
3 Sara came to _____ to study at Miss Minchin's school.

2 Circle the correct word.

1 When she arrived, Sara **liked** / **disliked** England.
2 Mr. Crewe had **one child** / **a lot of children**.
3 Miss Minchin **was** / **wasn't** interested in money.

3 What do you think happens in this story? Tick *Yes, Maybe* or *No* for each sentence.

	Yes	Maybe	No
1 Sara is a good student.	☐	☐	☐
2 Miss Minchin is very kind to her students.	☐	☐	☐
3 Sara's father loses all his money.	☐	☐	☐
4 Sara runs away from Miss Minchin's school.	☐	☐	☐

Extra reading 4

Aladdin

Many years ago, in a city in Arabia, there was a boy called Aladdin. He lived with his mother in a little house near the market, and they were very poor. Aladdin's mother worked all day, and sometimes half the night, but Aladdin never helped her.

He was a lazy boy and he did not like to work. He only wanted to play all the time. Every morning he ran through the streets to the market. There, he talked and laughed and played with his friends all day. Then in the evening he went home for his dinner.

And every night his mother said to him: "Oh, Aladdin, Aladdin! You are a lazy boy – a good-for-nothing! When are you going to do some work, my son?"

But Aladdin never listened to his mother.

One day in the market there was an old man in a long black coat. Aladdin did not see him, but the old man watched Aladdin very carefully. After

some minutes he went up to an orange-seller and asked:

"That boy in the green coat – who is he?"

"Aladdin, son of Mustafa," was the answer.

The old man moved away.

"Yes," he said quietly. "Yes, that is the boy. The right name, and the right father."

Then he called out to Aladdin: "Boy! Come here for a minute. Is your name Aladdin? Aladdin, son of Mustafa?"

Aladdin left his friends and came to the old man. "Yes," he said, "I am Aladdin, son of Mustafa. But my father is dead. He died five years ago."

"Dead!" said the old man. "Oh, no!" He put his face in his hands and began to cry.

"Why are you crying?" asked Aladdin. "Did you know my father?"

The old man looked up. "Mustafa was my brother!" he said. "I wanted to see him again, and now you tell me he is dead. Oh, this is not a happy day for me!" Then he put his hand on Aladdin's arm. "But here is my brother's son, and I can see Mustafa in your face, my boy. Aladdin, I am your uncle, Abanazar."

"My uncle?" said Aladdin. He was very surprised. "Did my father have a brother? I didn't know that."

"I went away before you were born, my boy," said the old man. "Look." He took ten pieces of gold out of his
bag, and put
them into
Aladdin's hands.
"Go home to
your mother
and give this

money to her. Tell her about me, and say this: Her husband's brother wants to meet her, and he is going to visit her tomorrow."

Ten pieces of gold is a lot of money and Aladdin was very happy. He ran home quickly and gave the gold to his mother. At first she was afraid.

"Where did you get this, Aladdin? Did you find it? It isn't our money. You must give it back."

"But it is our money, Mother," said Aladdin. "My uncle, my father's brother, gave the money to us. Uncle Abanazar is coming to visit us tomorrow."

"Who? You don't have an uncle Abanazar."

"But he knows my name, and my father's name," Aladdin said. "And he gave ten pieces of gold to me. He's very nice. You must make a good dinner for him."

The next day Abanazar arrived at Aladdin's house.

"My sister!" he said and smiled. "My dead brother's wife! I am happy to find you and Aladdin."

"Sit down, Abanazar. We're happy to see you in our poor home," Aladdin's mother said. She put meat, rice and fruit on the table. "But I don't understand. Why did my husband never speak about you?"

"I'm sorry, my sister. When we were young, my brother and I were not friends for many years. Then I went away to a far country. I am an old man now and wanted to see my brother again and take his hand. But he is dead, and I cannot speak to him or say goodbye to him now!"

Abanazar had tears in his eyes and Aladdin's mother began to cry too.

"But I am home again now," the old man said, "and I can help my brother's wife and his son, because I am a rich man." He looked at Aladdin. "Aladdin, my boy, what work do you do?"

Aladdin did not answer and his face was red.

"Oh, don't ask Aladdin questions about work!" his mother said. "He never works. He plays with his friends all day, and only comes home when he is hungry."

"Well, my boy, tomorrow we must get a new coat for you. Then we can talk about work. Would you like to have a shop in the market perhaps?"

Aladdin smiled. "A shop," he thought, "and me, a rich market-seller. Why not?"

1 Match the sentences with the people.

1 She's a poor woman. She works very hard.
2 He died five years ago. He was Aladdin's father.
3 He's a rich man. He wants to help Aladdin.
4 He's a lazy boy. He never does any work in the house.

a Aladdin
b Mustafa
c Aladdin's mother
d Abanazar

2 Fill in the blanks with the correct adjective below.

afraid   surprised   happy   sad

1 Aladdin was _____ when he met Abanazar. He didn't know he had an uncle.
2 Abanazar was _____ when Aladdin told him that Mustafa was dead.
3 Aladdin's mother was _____ when Aladdin gave her a lot of gold.
4 Abanazar was _____ when he met Aladdin and his mother.

3 What's going to happen in the story? Tick Yes, Maybe or No for each sentence.

	Yes	Maybe	No
1 Is Abanazar going to help Aladdin?	☐	☐	☐
2 Are Aladdin and his mother going to be rich?	☐	☐	☐
3 Is Aladdin going to marry a princess?	☐	☐	☐

Contents

Teachers' notes

Aims of this book

The aims of this book are:
- to show that all humans are built on the same basic pattern;
- to introduce the names of the main parts of the body and their functions;
- to show that humans vary and that we are all individuals;
- to provide a means of introducing basic ideas on health education;
- to form the foundation for simple ideas on genetics and evolution;
- to help children to understand that individual differences in rates of growth and development are quite normal.

Developing science skills

While it is not essential to follow the order of the worksheets, it is important that all those covering one aspect of a subject, such as the senses, are dealt with at approximately the same time.

It is important to remember that, although it is in the *doing* of science that children learn best, this involves more than just practical work. They need to observe, record, predict, measure, look for patterns, classify, explain and ask questions that can lead to further investigations. They need time to discuss their work, before and after the activity; this will also aid the teacher in monitoring the children's progress so that they build a valid framework for future development.

Safety precautions

The activities described on the worksheets mainly use everyday items of equipment and materials which are perfectly safe if used sensibly. Where extra care is necessary on safety grounds, this is mentioned both on the worksheets and also in the appropriate section of the teachers' notes.

There are two general safety precautions to take when teaching children about the workings of the human body. When discussing human variation, a particularly sensitive approach is needed when considering, for example, whether tall children have tall parents or whether blue-eyed parents have blue-eyed children. It is essential that children who are adopted, fostered, 'in care', or members of one-parent families, should not be made to feel unfortunate, abnormal, unusual or in any way different. It is also important that young children do not learn to associate any partss of their bodies with adult disapproval.

Scientific background

This information seeks to help you to understand the scientific concepts and ideas covered in this book. It generally goes beyond the level of understanding expected of most children, but will give you the confidence to ask and answer questions and to guide the children in their investigations.

The human species

People of all races, classes, colour or nationality belong to a single species, *Homo sapiens*. They share unique characteristics, such as a high degree of intelligence associated with a large, rounded skull, upright posture and the ability to communicate verbally.

Variation

Although no two people are alike (not even identical twins), all people have the same general body shape and the same internal structure. There are two broad types of variation. It is possible to arrange even a relatively small group of people into a continuous line – lightest to heaviest or tallest to shortest. Characteristics like these, in which there are many intermediates between the two extremes, are said to show continuous variation. Intelligence and human skin colour show continuous variation. The latter is due to a brown pigment, melanin, which protects the body from the harmful effects of the sun's rays. The different amounts of melanin in the skin cause the shade of colour of the various races.

Other characteristics have no, or very few, intermediate forms. People are, with rare exceptions, either male or female. They can or cannot roll their tongues into a U-shape. Everyone belongs to one of the four main blood groups.

Inheritance

An individual inherits characteristics from both parents, although what they are is due to chance. For example, she may inherit hair and eye colour from one or both parents, together with features such as the shape of the nose, ears and mouth. These hereditary characteristics are fixed from the moment or conception.

Environmental influences

Some of the traits we inherit can be altered by environmental influences, such as diet, activity, education, health and even wealth. Continuous variations are the ones most likely to be affected by the environment. The limit to a person's height, for example, is inherited, yet whether we achieve that potential maximum height depends on the nature of our diet, health and levels of exercise during the formative years.

Notes on individual activities

Page 5: Living and non-living

Key idea: there are differences between living and non-living things.
Likely outcome: living things: plant, earthworm, frog, child, tree, butterfly, dog. Non-living things: comb, television set, cup and saucer, motorcycle, teddy bear.
Developing the investigation: discuss living things – they feed, move, grow, breathe, excrete, reproduce and respond to changes. Do vehicles move because they are alive? Is a house under construction alive because it grows?

Page 6: A rainbow girl

Key idea: the parts of the body have their own individual names.
Developing the investigation: discuss the functions of the various parts of the body.

Page 7: A body game

Key idea: the parts of the body have their own names.
Extension activity: repeat this activity, naming parts of the head and face or parts of the limbs.

Page 8: Body measurements

Key idea: there are large variations among people in the measurements of parts of the body, even among children of similar age.
Developing the investigation: measure the variation in other parts of the body, such as head circumference and middle finger length.

Page 9: What I can do with my body

Key idea: we use different parts of the body for different activities.
Likely outcome: reading – hands and eyes; writing – hands and eyes; swimming, running, cycling and dancing – the whole body; watching television – the eyes and ears; listening to the radio – the ears.
Developing the investigation: discuss the value of physical exercise in strengthening the body.

Page 10: Your weight

Specialist equipment: bathroom scales.
Key idea: there is considerable variation in weight, even amongst children of similar ages.
Developing the investigation: use the bathroom scales to see how hard the children can push with one finger, one hand, both hands, one foot, both feet, and so on.

Page 11: Your face

Key idea: no two faces are exactly alike. Facial expressions are used to show moods or emotions.
Extension activity: ask the children to describe their likes and dislikes.

Page 12: Make face masks

Key idea: facial expressions are used to show moods or emotions.
Likely outcome: the children will probably have difficulty matching the mood of the character in their play to the appropriate facial expression.
Extension activity: devise a mime or a short play. Discuss the role of the eyes in facial expressions.

Page 13: Hair

Key idea: there is individual variation in hair colour, texture, thickness and strength.

Extension activity: do hairs from different people differ in appearance?

Page 14: Your teeth

Key idea: we have different numbers of teeth.
Likely outcome: a complete set of baby or milk teeth is 20. Adults have 32 teeth. The baby teeth normally start to loosen and fall out between the ages of six and twelve years. The biscuit will collect mainly in the crevices between the teeth and in the hollows and grooves at the tops of the back or 'double' teeth.
Extension activity: look at animals' teeth.

Page 15: Senses

Key idea: we have five main senses – sight, hearing, smell, touch and taste.
Likely outcome: you see with your eyes; you hear with your ears; smell with your nose; touch with your hands (or, more accurately, your skin); taste with your tongue. Sight is used the most. When eating food, we use our senses of sight, touch, taste and smell.
Extension activity: discuss how our senses keep us safe.

Page 16: Tongues

Key idea: tongue size and shape varies from individual to individual. Tongue rolling is an inherited characteristic; it cannot be learned unless the ability is already present.
Likely outcome: no amount of practice will turn a non-tongue-roller into someone with that ability.
Developing the investigation: devise ways of showing the vital role of the tongue in speech.
Extension activity: survey how many people have lobed bases to their ears and how many have ears with no distinct lobe (another characteristic).

Page 17: Eyes

Key idea: eye colour varies from individual to individual. It is an inherited characteristic.
Extension activity: examine the pupils of the eyes in bright and dim light.

Page 18: Can we believe our eyes?

Key idea: our eyes can sometimes deceive us.
Extension activity: look at coloured objects, first indoors under fluorescent lights, then outside. Do the colours always appear the same?

Page 19: Food

Key idea: we need a variety of foods if we are to grow, be active and stay healthy.
Developing the investigation: make block graphs or pie charts of favourite foods.
Extension activity: look at proteins, carbohydrates and fats, vitamins and mineral salts.

Page 20: Food from animals and plants

Key idea: some of our foods come from animals, others from plants.
Developing the investigation: discuss the origins of common foods, such as bread, eggs and milk.

Page 21: The skeleton

Key idea: The human body is supported by a skeleton of bones.
Likely outcome: the longest individual bones are the leg bones; the shortest that the children can feel are the individual finger and toe bones, although the three tiny bones inside each ear are even smaller.
Developing the investigation: discuss what our bodies would be like if we did not have bones. Compare with those of animals which lack a skeleton, such as earthworms and jellyfish.

Page 22: Joints

Key idea: joints enable the bones to move.
Developing the investigation: discuss where else joints can be found besides in the human body.
Extension activity: show the children a string puppet.

Page 23: Listen to your heartbeat

Key idea: the heart is a kind of pump which drives blood around the body.
Likely outcome: during and after exercise the heart will beat faster than it did when at rest.
Developing the investigation: discuss what the blood does (carries food, oxygen and heat to all parts of the body, removes waste and helps to fight germs).
Safety precautions: all children doing this activity must be physically fit. No child who is excused games or PE activities on medical grounds should be allowed to be the subject of this activity.

Page 24: Breathing

Key ideas: we breathe air to stay alive. We breathe faster during exercise than when at rest.
Extension activity: discuss air pollution and breathing, and air and burning.
Safety precautions: all children doing this activity must be physically fit. No child who is excused games or PE activities on medical grounds should be allowed to carry out this activity.

Page 25: Growing

Key ideas: growth involves changes to the shape and size of the body. The size and styles of our clothing change as we grow older.
Extension activity: compare the handprints of a child and an adult.

Page 26: You as a baby

Key idea: important physical and mental

changes take place between babyhood and childhood.
Developing the investigation: discuss the prolonged care involved in bringing up a baby.

Page 27: Me and my friends

Key idea: a comparison of individual differences.
Extension activity: discuss all the different people involved in keeping children safe and happy.

Page 28: How good is your memory?

Key idea: some people are better at remembering things than others.
Extension activity: see if older children can remember short sequences of numbers or letters. Can memory be improved with practice?

Page 29: Which side of your body do you use the most?

Key idea: people differ in their preference for their right or left hands and other body parts.

Developing the investigation: encourage the children to write or draw with their 'wrong' hand for a few minutes. Do they find it difficult?
Extension activity: devise some more tests to see which foot people prefer to use.

Page 30: Handprints

Key idea: the size, shape and pattern of handprints varies from person to person.
Extension activity: compare foot sizes.

Page 31: Measuring hands

Key idea: simple methods of measuring the area and carrying capacity of the hands.
Extension activity: discuss the advantages of standard units of measurement.

Page 32: All about me

Key idea: a summary of qualities and differences.
Extension activity: find out some famous people.

National Curriculum: Science

These pages support the following requirements of the National Curriculum for Science.

AT2 – Pupils should:
• find out about themselves and develop their ideas about how they grow, feed, move, use their senses and about the stages of human development.
• consider similarities and differences between themselves and other pupils, and understand that individuals are unique.

AT3 – Pupils should:
• collect and find similarities and differences between a variety of everyday materials.

AT4 – Pupils should:
• have opportunities to explore light sources and the effects related to shadow, reflection and colour.

Scottish 5-14 Curriculum: Environmental studies

Attainment outcome	Strand
Science in the environment	Living things – plants and animals including humans; their distinctive features and characteristics Forces – different types of force involved in moving and stopping Energy – different forms, sources and uses Processes of life – conditions for life and growth; life cycles, key life processes such as breathing and movement
Healthy and safe living	Relationships – relationships and feelings, and their influence on behaviour, responsibility Looking after myself – ways of keeping healthy, growth and change, feelings, choices
Investigating	Finding out – implementing plans, using the senses, instruments, measuring devices, books and documents Recording – recording findings in words, diagrams, sketches, graphs
Designing and making	Making – implementing plans; organising and using equipment, materials and workspace effectively Evaluating – commenting on appearances and effectiveness of creations; making modifications

▲ Name _____

Living and non-living

You will need: a pencil; coloured pencils or crayons.

▲ Look at the pictures. Which of them are of living things?
▲ Colour the living things.

▲ Using the back of this page, make a list of some more living things.

A rainbow girl

You will need: a pencil; coloured pencils or crayons.

▲ Using coloured pencils or crayons, colour the drawing of a girl in the following way.
- Colour the hair red.
- Colour the arms orange.
- Colour the hands yellow.
- Colour the body green.
- Colour the legs blue.
- Colour the feet purple.

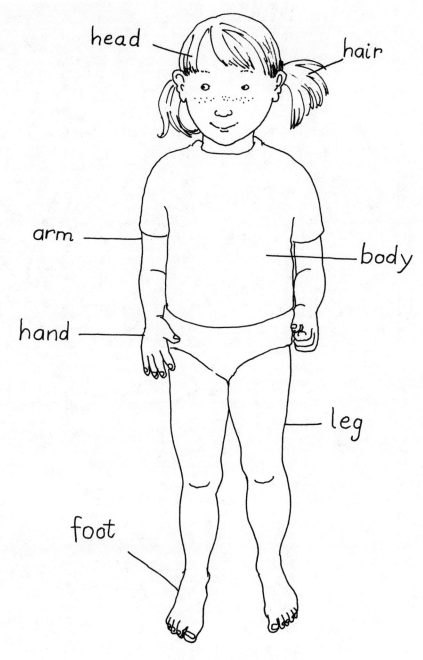

▲ Now draw and colour a rainbow boy.

A body game

You will need: a toy brick; small pictures of parts of the body; glue; a pencil.

Work with some friends.

▲ Stick a small picture on each side of the brick. Then roll the brick. Can your friend name the part of the body that lands face up? Now try this with other friends. Who knows the most parts of the body?

▲ Draw a picture of yourself. Label the parts of your body.

▲ Name _____

Body measurements

You will need: a tape measure; a pencil.

Work with a friend.

▲ Measure how tall you are.   I am _____ cm high.

▲ Measure your hand-span.   My hand-span is _____ cm.

▲ Measure your foot.   My foot is _____ cm long.

▲ Measure your arm-span.   My arm-span is _____ cm.

▲ Now measure your friend. Are your friend's measurements the same as yours?

What I can do with my body

You will need: a pencil.

▲ Look at these pictures. Say which part of your body you use for each of these activities. Choose from: hands, legs, head, eyes, ears and your whole body.

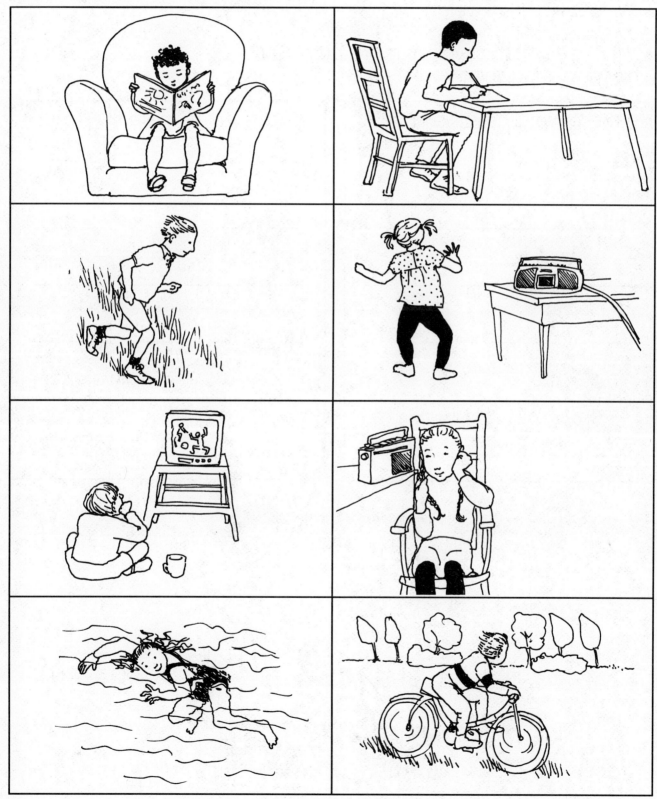

Your weight

You will need: bathroom scales; a pencil.

▲ When you were born you weighed about 4 kilogrammmes.
How much do you weigh now? Stand on the scales and see.

▲ Write it like this: I weigh _____ kilogrammes.

▲ Who in your class weighs more than you?
Who weighs less than you?

These weigh less then me:		These weigh more then me:	
Name	Weight	Name	Weight
_____	_____	_____	_____
_____	_____	_____	_____
_____	_____	_____	_____
_____	_____	_____	_____
_____	_____	_____	_____

Your face

You will need: a mirror; a pencil.

▲ Look at your face in the mirror. Draw your face in this shape.

▲ Label as many parts as you can.

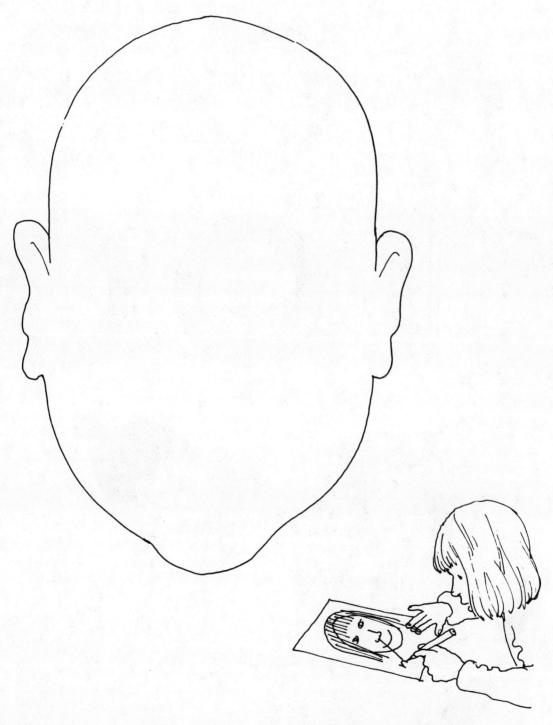

▲ Draw how you would look if you were happy, sad, angry or surprised.

Make face masks

You will need: paper plates; sticks; glue; a pencil; coloured pencils or crayons.

▲ Draw some faces on the plates.

▲ Glue two plates together with the stick wedged between them.

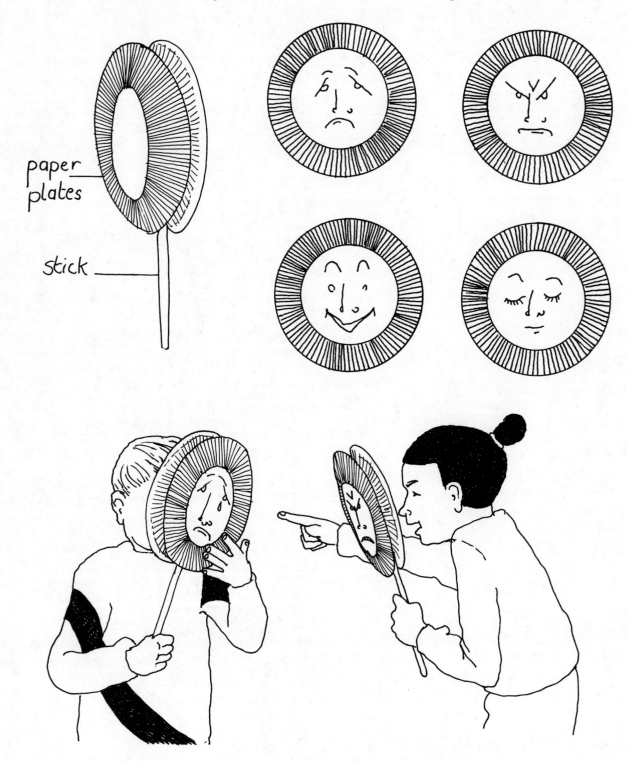

paper
plates

stick

▲ Make a mask play. Tell the story using the right faces.

Hair

You will need: a long hair; sticky tape; paper; paper-clips; a pencil.

▲ What colour is your hair? Is it brown, black, red or fair?

My hair is _____

▲ How strong is a hair? Fix a long hair like in the picture below with a paper loop on the end. Put paper-clips, one at a time, into the loop of paper attached to the hair.

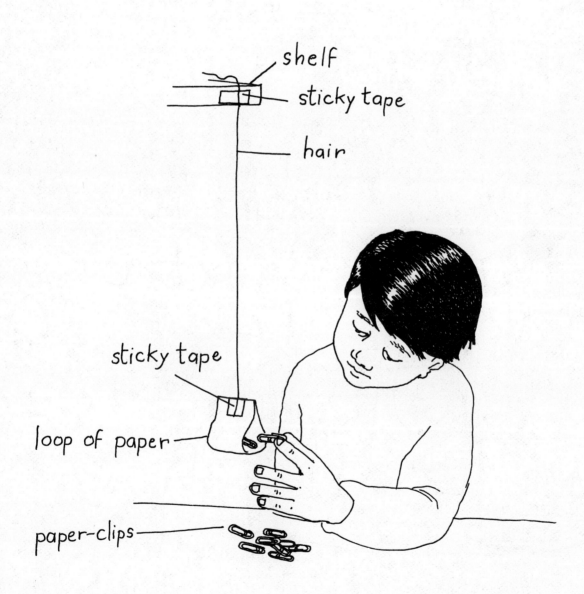

▲ Try this again with a hair from someone else.

▲ Name _____

Your teeth

You will need: a small mirror; a chocolate biscuit; coloured pencils; a pencil.

▲ Look in the mirror at your teeth. Colour the tooth chart to show your teeth. How many teeth do you have altogether?

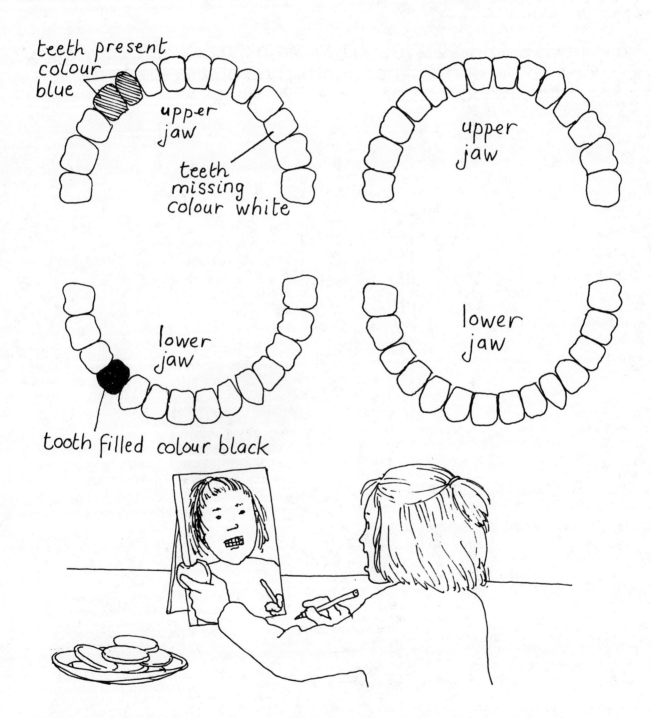

▲ Chew the chocolate biscuit and look in the mirror. Where does the chocolate collect? Show these places on your chart.
▲ Why should we clean our teeth after meals?

Senses

You will need: a pencil; a ruler.

▲ You have five senses. Match the sentence with the right part of the body.

• You see with your

• You hear with your

• You smell with your

• You touch with your

• You taste with your

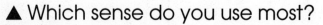

▲ Which sense do you use most?

▲ Which senses do you use when eating your food?

Tongues

You will need: a mirror; a pencil.

▲ Is everyone's tongue the same? Look in the mirror.
Is your tongue round or pointed?

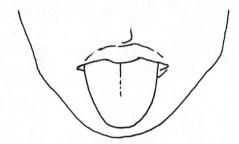 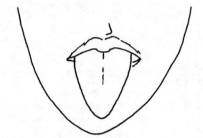

▲ Can you touch your nose with your tongue?

▲ Can you roll your tongue like this?

▲ Make a chart like this.
Say what your tongue and your friends' tongues are like.

Name	Round or pointed	Can roll tongue	Can touch nose with tongue

Eyes

You will need: a mirror; a pencil.

▲ Look in the mirror. Look at your eyes.

Can you see the parts shown in the picture?

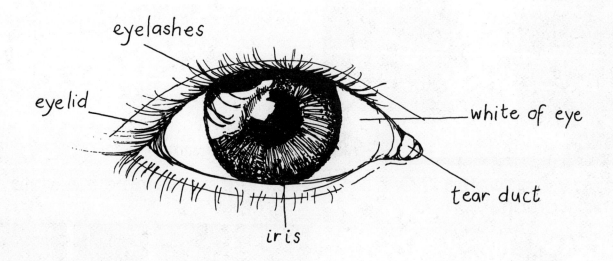

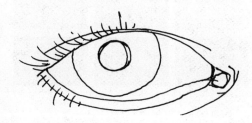

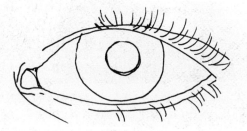

▲ Colour the picture.

▲ Are your friends' eyes the same colour as yours?

Can we believe our eyes?

You will need: a pencil; a ruler.

▲ Look carefully at the pictures. Can we always believe what we see?

Is this a vase? Or is it two faces?

Is this a rabbit? Or is it a duck?

Is this a young woman? Or is it an old woman?

Are there spots where the white lines cross?

Which flower centre is larger?

Food

You will need: a pencil; a ruler.

Some foods give us energy.

Some foods help to us grow.

Some foods keep us healthy.

▲ Which of these foods have you eaten today?

_____

_____

▲ Which foods do you like the best?

_____

_____

▲ Colour the foods that keep us healthy.

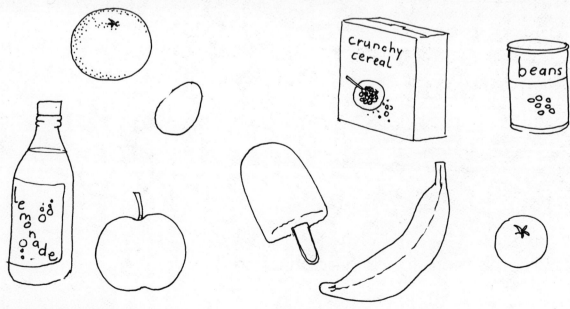

Food from animals and plants

You will need: a pencil.

Some of our food comes from animals.

Some of our food comes from plants.

▲ Draw some more foods in each circle.

The skeleton

You will need: a tape measure.

▲ Look at this picture of a skeleton. It is made up of bones.
▲ Can you feel your bones?
▲ Measure some of your bones.

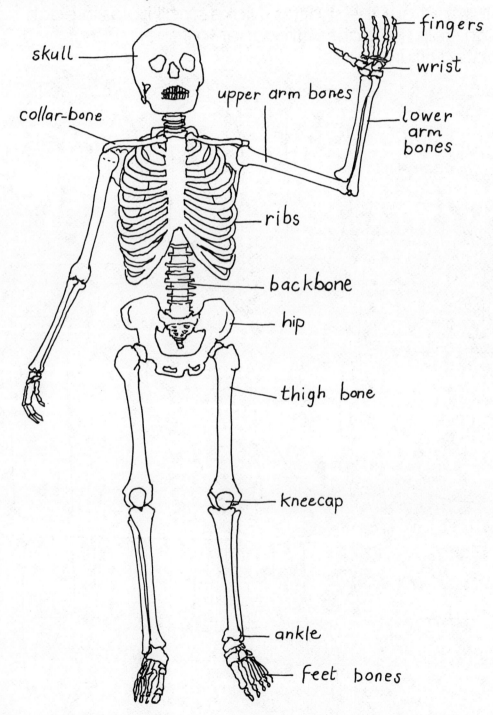

skull

fingers

wrist

upper arm bones

collar-bone

lower arm bones

ribs

backbone

hip

thigh bone

kneecap

ankle

feet bones

▲ Which is the longest bone you can find? Which is the shortest?

Joints

You will need: thin card; scissors; paper fasteners; glue.

We can move because we have joints. Joints are places where two bones meet.

▲ Make this jointed figure. Stick the shapes below on to thin card. Carefully cut out the shapes. Make small holes in each part as shown. Join the parts with paper fasteners. Play with your jointed figure.

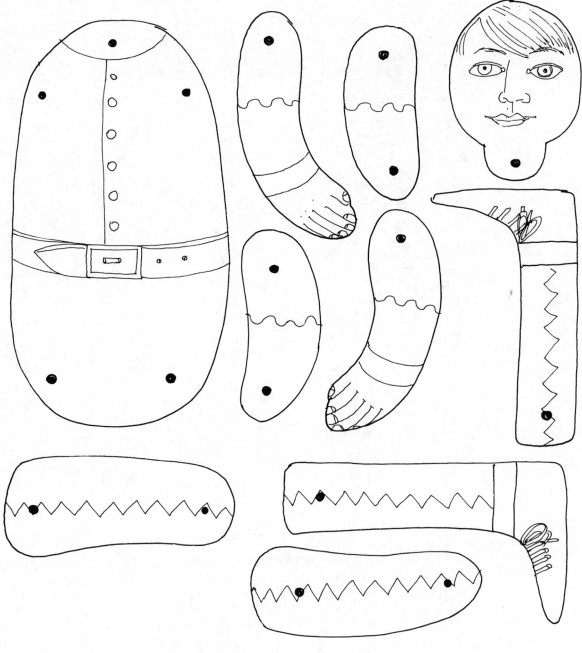

▲ How many of these joints can you find on your body?
▲ Are there any joints on your body which are not on the figure?

Listen to your heartbeat

You will need: a tube; two plastic funnels; a pencil.

▲ Put the funnels in the tube like this. Listen to your heartbeat.
Run around the playground. Listen again. Sit still and listen again.
What do you notice?

plastic or rubber tube

funnel

Breathing

You will need: a pencil.

Living things breathe. They need air to stay alive. You breathe all the time. You breathe air to keep you alive.

▲ Put your hands on your chest. Breathe in. Can you feel your chest move? Breathe out. Can you feel your chest move?

▲ Now run around the playground. Put your hands on your chest again. Do you breathe faster or slower? How can you find out?

Growing

You will need: a pencil.

As we grow, we get bigger. It takes time to grow.

▲ Look at these children.

Caroline is 6 months old.
Petra is 6 years old.
Kevin is 14 years old.
Sanjit is 1 year old.
Kirsty is 2 years old.

▲ Write each of the children's names under their picture.

▲ Draw some of the clothes Caroline might wear.
▲ Draw some of the clothes Petra might wear.

You as a baby

You will need: a pencil.

▲ Find out all you can about yourself when you were a baby.

When were you born? _____

Where were you born? _____

How much did you weigh?_____

What was your hair like?_____

When did you first walk?_____

What was your first word? _____

What toys did you play with?_____

Have you a picture of yourself when you were a baby?

Me and my friends

You will need: a pencil; a tape measure; bathroom scales.

Work with some friends.

▲ Fill in this chart.

name	boy or girl	age	hair colour	height	weight

▲ Can you find anyone exactly like you?

How good is your memory?

You will need: a pencil; a clock with a second hand.

How much can you remember?

▲ Look carefully at this picture for one minute. Now cover the picture. How many of the things can you remember in two minutes? Write them down.

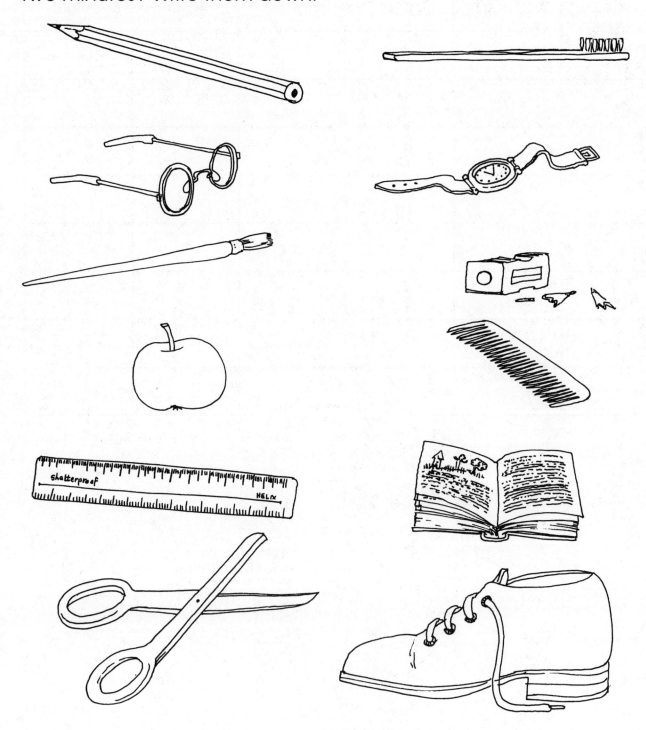

▲ Who has the best memory in your class?

Which side of your body do you use the most?

You will need: a pen.

▲ Are you left-handed or right-handed? Pick up a pen and see.

▲ Scratch your back. Which hand do you use?

▲ Cup your hand to hear better. Which ear do you use?

▲ Wink at someone. Which eye do you use?

▲ Tilt your head on your shoulder. Which shoulder does your head touch?

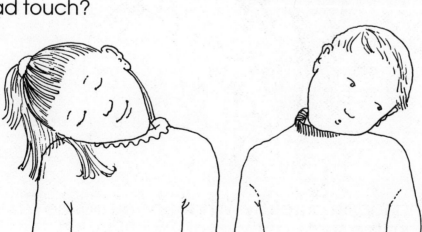

Handprints

You will need: newspapers; a large, flat sponge; poster paint; paper; water; a pencil.

▲ Make some handprints. Mix the poster paint until it is runny. Soak the sponge on a thick layer of newspaper. Press your hand down on the sponge. Then press your hand on a clean sheet of paper.

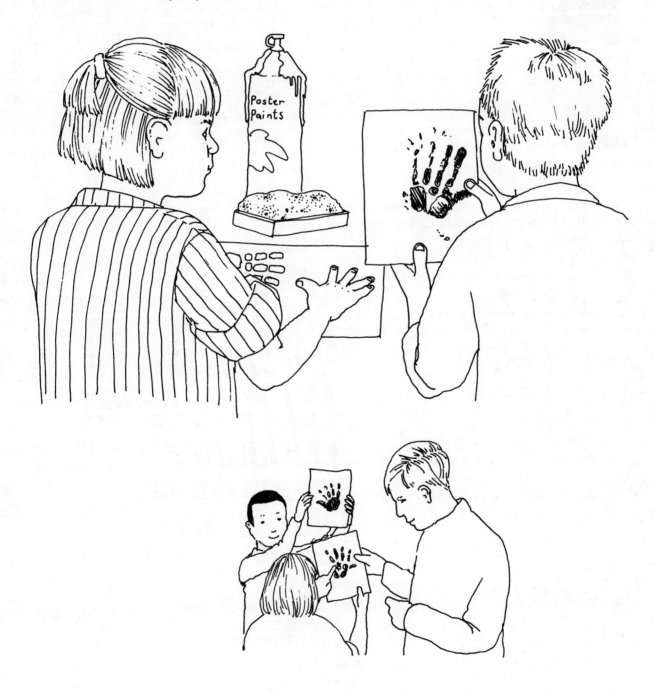

▲ Look at your handprint carefully. What do you notice?
▲ Is your handprint the same as those of your friends?

Measuring hands

You will need: some squared paper; beads or marbles; a pencil.

▲ Put your hand on the paper. Draw round your hand. Count the squares in your hand picture. (Do not count very small parts of a square.)

Write down: My hand covers _____ squares.

▲ Here is another way of measuring your hand. See how many marbles you can pick up with it.

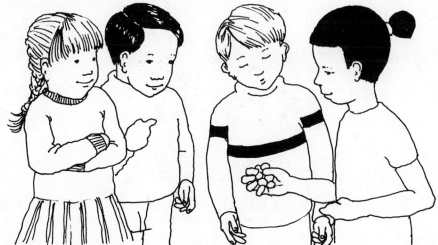

▲ Who has the biggest hands in your class?_____

▲ Whose hands are the smallest?_____

All about me

You will need: a pencil; glue; scissors; paper.

▲ Make a book about yourself. Call it 'All about Me'.
Stick some pictures of yourself in it. Put your fingerprints,
handprints and footprints in it. Write down this information
about yourself.

My height _____ My weight_____

The colour of my eyes _____ The colour of my hair _____

My favourite food _____ My favourite drink_____

My favourite animal_____ My favourite sport_____

My favourite television programme _____

My favourite colour _____

My favourite singer_____

▲ Compare your book with those of your friends.
Is there anyone else exactly like you?